MOUNTAIN BIKING

SPORTS CHALLENGE

DAVID ARMENTROUT

The Rourke Book Co., Inc.
Vero Beach, Florida 32964

David Armentrout specializes in nonfiction writing and has had several book series published for primary schools. He resides in Cincinnati with his wife and two children.

PHOTO CREDITS:
© Mike Powell/Allsport: page 4; © Nathan Bilow/Allsport: page 12; © Tim Defrisco/Allsport: pages 15, 22; © Allsport: page 21; © Kirk Anderson/Intl Stock: Cover; © Eric Sanford/Intl Stock: pages 6, 13; © Robin Schwartz/Intl Stock: page 7; © Tony Demin/Intl Stock: page 10; © G. Bigham/Intl Stock: page 16; © Chuck Mason/Intl Stock: page 18; © Chad Ehlers/Intl Stock: page 19; © Kim Karpeles: page 9

EDITORIAL SERVICES:
Penworthy Learning Systems

Library of Congress Cataloging-in-Publication Data

Armentrout, David, 1962 -
    Mountain biking / by David Armentrout.
        p. cm. — (Sports challenge)
    Includes index.
    Summary: Presents basic information on the essential skills, techniques, and equipment for mountain biking.
    ISBN 1-55916-219-8
    1. All terrain cycling—Juvenile literature. [1. All terrain cycling.]
I. Title II. Series: Armentrout, David, 1962 -   Sports challenge.
GV1056.A76 1997
796.6'3—dc21   97–12419
                                                                    CIP
                                                                    AC

Printed in the USA

TABLE OF CONTENTS

Mountain Biking

People of all ages ride mountain bikes. Sometimes referred to as an **all-terrain bike** (AWL tur RAYN BYK), a mountain bike's sturdy construction allows people to ride off-road on rough ground.

Mountain biking does not mean you have to take your bike up steep hills or down rocky paths. People ride mountain bikes on paved bike paths and city streets as well as on rugged dirt trails. This flexibility is one reason why mountain biking is one of the most popular sports.

Off-road racing tests a rider's skill and speed.

THE MOUNTAIN BIKE

A mountain bike is recognized by its fat tires, which absorb shock. Flat handle bars also distinguish mountain bikes from other bikes. They can be adjusted to give a rider correct posture.

A mountain bike's fat tires help absorb shock when riding on bumpy terrain.

A mountain bike's lightweight frame makes it easy to carry.

The sturdy, but lightweight, frame, or main structure of the bike, consists of joined tubes. Other parts of the bike, like the seat post, wheels, gear system, brake system, and steering system, all attach to the frame.

THE RIGHT BIKE FOR YOU

You will need to consider many things before choosing a mountain bike. How much money are you willing to spend? Will you be riding on dirt trails, rocky hills, paved roads, or on snowy slopes? Will you take your bike on all these surfaces?

You should consider the width of the tires, the type of seat, and the braking system.

Most importantly, find the right size bike for your body. When you visit a bike shop, ask for help and try out many styles for size and comfort.

Mountain bikes come in many sizes and styles.

SAFETY GEAR AND CLOTHING

The bike helmet is the most important piece of safety equipment. It is made to protect your head from serious injury. You need to buy one with a proper fit and wear it all the time while riding.

Your clothing should be comfortable and absorbent. Close-fitting clothes are best because they won't get caught in the moving parts of the bike. Long sleeves will protect your arms from branches, and gloves protect your hands and help grip the handlebars.

Wear comfortable clothing and a safety helmet when bike riding.

TRAIL RIDING

Trail riding (TRAYL RYD ing) is very popular. Not everyone can, or wants to, ride up and down steep rocky hillsides or compete in races.

Trail riding can still get you on some challenging terrain. It also gets you away from busy city streets and highways and into quiet natural settings.

Fat tires with tough tread help grip loose dirt.

Mountain bikes can be ridden in all kinds of weather.

State tourism departments, commerce centers, and parks and recreation departments can give you information about the places where mountain biking is allowed.

OFF-ROAD RACING

Off-road racing tests a rider's skill and speed. The rider with the fastest time wins the race. Some of the events are called downhill, **dual slalom** (DOO ul SLAH lum), and hill climbs.

The downhill races are often on dirt paths or rocky hillsides. Sometimes, though, a steep, snowy hill is the challenging terrain.

A dual slalom race pairs riders side by side on separate courses. They have to control their bikes around **obstacles** (AHB stuh kulz), or gates, while moving at tremendous speed.

A Colorado ski resort is used for mountain bike competition during the summer.

OTHER COMPETITIONS

The cross-country race is also about speed. Riders compete on a difficult course and never ride the same area twice. The cross-country mountain bike race made its Olympic debut in the 1996 Atlanta Summer Games.

Observed trials (ub ZERVD TRY ulz) is an event that takes riders over obstacles like holes, logs, and boulders. Completing the course without setting a foot on the ground is the goal of this competition. If a foot touches the ground, points are gathered. The rider with the lowest number of points wins the race.

It takes balance and skill to compete in observed trials.

Riding Rules

Mountain bikers must follow the rules of the road, or trail, just as hikers, horseback riders, and automobile drivers do. Riding to school or the store means following traffic laws. Trail riding means respecting the natural beauty of the trail as well as the other bikers using it.

Bike riding is enjoyed by people of all ages.

Mountain biking is a great way to explore the countryside.

Overnight trips are fun but may require contacting park rangers or other authorities. Dry conditions may mean no camp fires. If conditions are too wet or too dry, mountain bikes may be banned.

BMX

The letters **BMX** (BEE em EKS) stand for bicycle motocross. It is a sport that grabs the attention of many young riders. BMXers race around a dirt track while hitting bumps and jumping ramps.

A BMX bike has a smaller frame than the mountain bike and only a single gear. A bike's tough bumpy tires—called **knobbies** (NAHB eez)—grip loose dirt. The high v-shaped handlebars have protective padding.

For those riders who like to show off, there is BMX freestyle. No dirt track is used, just controlled tricks performed with a BMX freestyle bike.

BMX riders scramble for the lead around a dirt track.

GLOSSARY

all-terrain bike (AWL tuh RAYN BYK) — a bike
suitable for any surface

BMX (BEE em EKS) — bicycle motorcross; a
bicycle race on a bumpy dirt track with ramps
and other obstacles

dual slalom (DOO ul SLAH lum) — two sloping
courses side-by-side that have obstacles to
zigzag around

knobbies (NAHB eez) — tires with small bumps
or knobs on them that grip the ground

observed trials (ub ZERVD TRY ulz) — a
mountain biking competition where course
observers watch the riders and add points when a
rider's foot touches the ground during the event

obstacles (AHB stuh kulz) — things that get in
the way

trail riding (TRAYL RYD ing) — riding a bike
off-road for pleasure

BMX is a challenging sport for young riders.

INDEX